THE COMMUNITY CLASSROOM

THE COMMUNITY CLASSROOM

AVERY NIGHTINGALE

CONTENTS

Copyright © 2024 by Avery Nightingale
All rights reserved. No part of this book may be reproduced in any manner whatsoever without written permission except in the case of brief quotations embodied in critical articles and reviews.
First Printing, 2024

CHAPTER 1

Introduction

In life, learning is witnessed through various informal settings. Researchers have come out to say that through these informal settings, learning can occur opportunistically while the people are in action. Being social creatures, our learning is always intertwined with what we love to do most, where we gain through association as we educate each other.

This colloquium session will therefore bring sisal farmers and the farmers' children together in one classroom to learn mathematics. The environment will be extended to a more social space on the farming grounds where they live through the community classroom. This will coincide with issues that researchers in developing societies have long been arguing for a human-centric system. The term human centrism is coined to challenge the pervasive influence of technology in many room-based systems in educational learning.

The University of Kwazulu-Natal can be counted as one of the institutions that has embraced a human-centric system by extending the learning of mathematics to a community. The community classroom concept is one of the less room-centric learning approaches that include connectedness to other people in terms of understanding and application of what is learned. The researchers' motivation is derived from the fact that these children are situated in a social setting where learning is supported by the presence of elders and peers. This demographic is perceived by the government and education stakeholders in general as agents of change in low-income rural setups. This research therefore unveils some of the views that can enrich thinking on what good education may look like, especially in the less resourced locations.

CHAPTER 2

Benefits of Community Learning

Children who grow up in institutions do not develop a similar sense of continuity with the past. They live in a continuous present with no sense of drama or use for anything that happened before their individual births. And schools contribute actively to building a cyclopean present. When several generations share the same space and when several generations interact keenly with one another, the benefits are not confined to children alone. In many 'respect for the past' societies, old people used to play important roles in the kinds of wisdom that would outlast individual human lives. In less traditional times, people don't have time for stories, especially from those too old to be of much practical use any longer. Storytelling was not necessarily about folklore or heritage, but simply a means for each age group to celebrate its successes, mourn its failures and share its discoveries with others.

One of the most powerful aspects of learning in a community context is that a person can build on the outcomes and learnings of previous generations. Trudging up the hill towards the school, a girl stopped me - she wanted to know why the sparrows of the village never stopped to peck in my courtyard. This was not a part of her school syllabus. It was something that I had shared with a previous batch of children visiting my home as part of their study of nature. Although sparrows seem to be shunning all human habitations these days, they had been common birds around most houses a decade ago. I told the girl so. She went back to a world where sparrows could still be seen around people's homes and trees, plants and caterpillars were some of the other elements of that world. A world that was not too long gone. She would not take it for granted that things would always be the same for whatever life forms still shared space with humans.

Enhanced Knowledge Sharing

The top-down transmission of information to teachers often makes students seem disempowered. However, in addition to learning directly from all peers and having at least a voice, the new Community Class system repositions the expertise from being entirely top-heavy. This makes it possible for all interests or chapters to have a speaker. With a number of group discussions and the forum on their own only, some active interest also often persisted in additional activities in the field. Although, in an active approach, pity arises the possibility for instructors and students to take on the role of a peer mentor. Integrative learning difficulties have shown that the lack of comprehension and deep rumination has been a difficult obstacle to student learning. Scientists have demonstrated the growing contribution of educators to manual application of problem-solving methods. Rather than promoting the hyper-technical acceptance of career education, the study challenges the promotion of such innovative practices and demonstrates the use of training as a medium for life and self-improvement. The symposium also gives psychological encouragement.

One of the principal promising aspects brought about by the Community Classroom is that of the expansion of the knowledge-sharing process. The extent of this enhancement is as vast as the diverse and unique ways in which the system is employed. Whether as a primary means of education, interactive learning, a means of continued instruction, or for the establishment of links with foreign educational institutions, the new digital class documented success in knowledge transfer and increased student engagement. Just as casual conversations can optimize the educational activity by allowing teachers to monitor the classroom actively, the class also encourages student habits in communication, critical thinking, and the explication of reasoning during systematic discussions. Studies confirm that such practices can enhance lifelong learning and self-improvement.

Increased Motivation and Engagement

Increased motivation and engagement are evident across a range of qualitative and quantitative measures. By also capturing the degree of participant interaction via the frequency and content of their interactions, we show that increasing interactivity by providing learners the opportunity to give and receive feedback from their peers using methods like the communal crux, compared to learners who worked individually and submitted more solutions. Additionally, learners who were made aware that their solutions have appeared to more solvers were better connected to the larger network, compared to their counterparts. Threshold concepts in any content area are ideas or concepts that are challenging for students to understand but also foundational to their further learning. It is necessary to identify threshold concepts to better understand areas of struggle as well, in order to provide appropriate instructional support to learners that is required. The literature suggests that identifying such threshold concepts and misconceptions prior to the instruction is indeed key without wanting to spend that VPN to address more effectively and to reduce the size.

How can learners be motivated to persevere through delays in receiving feedback in a community classroom? We began by exploring the concept of future audience, whose support and engagement was hypothesized to motivate learners to persevere in large, massive learning environments. To test this hypothesis, we exposed learners in a MOOC to others in the course, i.e., to their immediate community, who would indeed look at and prove or disprove learners' solutions, offering feedback for the learner and engaging with the content. Over a period of 16 days, learners had the opportunity to provide feedback and solve each other's problems using this inverted classroom. Our preliminary investigation revealed some promising results. Through the availability of feedback of their solutions from different viewpoints and your peers [a study participant], you do get very motivated to consider a more creative and diverse set of solutions to a given problem. In fact, two-thirds of learners considered altogether more diverse solution sets (more unique ideas) when comparing their first to second replies.

Diverse Perspectives and Experiences

"We - the students and the mentors - are not different people on different sides of the table either, but we are all bound by mutual struggles and triumphs that warrant our curious thoughts and loving hearts. It is undoubtedly the power of education that has enabled our growth and friendship magnificently," stated Tharice. Upon returning home, the students expressed a range of misconceptions and confusion. Phally exited a car at dusk and looked on both sides of the street with confusion; "I think I forgot that all stores close at 5 pm, this is still weird to me," lamented Phally. Saroeun opened the mysterious dishwasher, even after living here for a month, and asked Tina, a mentor and former Fulbright Scholar, to explain the science behind it. Complex concepts such as the dishwasher left her as puzzled as when she discussed similar confounding topics with Tina back home in Cambodia. So naturally, all mentors try our best in every lesson and make efforts in every trip we took to make each individual student comfortable and establish their familiar work routine again.

The first day of the community classroom was filled with excitement and nerves. As we introduced ourselves, the diversity of perspectives was immediately apparent. As many of us grew up outside of the United States and had different opportunities, most of us wanted to learn more about American culture as a part of our English immersion program. "I hope to learn more about my new environment and different perspectives by interacting with members of the community," said Stellah. While the students were mostly young adults, all survivors of armed conflict and extreme poverty, the mentors were a diverse group: a college volunteer, a social worker, and a mental health professional. "I came to this program because I want to give back to vulnerable survivors that didn't have the same privilege I had," shared Tina, a former Fulbright scholar from Cambodia. Similarly, Huy, a Vietnamese-American and aspiring teacher, volunteered to help the students access and navigate the educational system in Iowa City. Mark, a social worker at the Center, wraps up our age range - he brings a fun personality, a wealth of relevant experience and many colorful bow-ties to the classroom each week. With our wide-ranging personalities, interests, and backgrounds, we've been able to support and learn from each other in a most remarkable way.

CHAPTER 3

Setting Up a Community Classroom

The birth of the compilation course started in response to a freshman's question in a language and tran... he truths are now (or what is thought to be). How should society be repaid in return for the particularly long years of education that society longs for as a goal by sending the pros and cons of each animal? My students, now that society is like that, because society is something that is composed of people, the only thing we can do for people is to move. I think the action that is present there is to interact, accept each other, and have people understand the other person. I think this is the most important value for humans to have, but I would like to consider some kind of lifestyle and future plans to help make people bigger. We received a very clear answer that "it is up to the pros and cons to interact and pay respect to each other that society will be repaid".

The classroom consists of about 200 students, both from the community classroom and from a host institution (an elementary school in this case). Typically, the majority of students are freshmen who take a certain class that only gives two credits before the semester begins. The activities were divided into three main categories: everyday interaction, which includes conversations such as "art studios" created on classroom tables and daily interaction at lunch and on the way home, and an hour of group activities at the end of a three-hour class.

Compared to other types of service-learning, a community classroom emphasizes the indoctrination of service. It is designed to benefit faculty and students while providing valuable services and creating an interaction space for participants of various ages and groups. In the typical community classroom environment, the roles of recipients and benefactors of the service are reversed. All participants are both recipients and benefactors.

Identifying Learning Goals

They describe the former as related to what each learner should have by the end of the educational process, while the teacher goals are short-term sub-targets leading learners to the standard goals; these are internal outcomes and elements to be achieved by the learners. Lastly, there are course aims, which are the kinds of knowledge, items to be remembered, skills one should acquire and habits that should be adopted. Teachers have the duty to have great intimacy with the learning goals in guiding them to fulfillment—think of a possible compromising scenario in intimate relationship such as this. That direction will provide learners with a clear direction in class. Teachers, no doubt, work genuinely and alter behaviors to produce the change in the future, such as an object that is attracted to a gravitational center, altering the orbit of a celestial body.

Learning goals, then, are the foundation of our teaching. They are the guideline for all the choices we will have to make along the way, the things we must do to fulfill our mission. We want specific responses from the learners at the end of the instruction. To know that those responses are the desired ones, it is necessary to examine them to make sure they include measurable and observable behaviors. The conditions under which the learners will give them also have to be set, as well as the criteria by which learners will be evaluated. Instructional designers have many ways to communicate the learners what they are accomplishing throughout the learning process or what they have to do to realize they are progressing in the right direction, or even whether they are falling short of the expectations. They can do so using the information about the learners' achievement. proposed three kinds of requirements: subjects' standards, teacher goals and course aims.

Creating a Supportive Environment

In August 2004, we received a PowerPoint presentation sent out by our CEO, designed as a discussion piece for her staff upon their return from summer break. The ten pages had two pictures on them that caught our eyes. The first was labeled "A Traditional Classroom" and had a picture of a classroom filled with desks, with children working solo. The second was labeled "The Community Classroom" and had a picture of a messy classroom with everyone involved working together in groups. The message was clear – look around, we don't work with traditional children, so we can't employ traditional strategies. We needed to work together as a team to teach all the children, regardless of the functional unit of operation – be it a classroom, the school, or the entire organization.

Today, much of the support that was given as a matter of course in the past has vanished. Poverty, substance abuse, violence, and many other challenges are often the defining experiences of our students' childhood. Our community was created to provide children in need with learning resources not readily available to them otherwise. So, as you can see, we work with a very challenging audience. Add to it our resource limitations as an organization and the challenge of an annual 1/3 staff turnover rate that characterizes many urban schools, we face significant challenges in creating that safe, supportive environment that is conducive to learning. We will not allow our decisions to isolate us from the staff that has a unique position in understanding their individual students' needs.

In the past, creating a safe and supportive environment for children was easy. Life was organized around the family, and children could grow up learning from the time-tested wisdom that was handed down from generation to generation. The family was supported by a network of extended family members, friends, and community organizations that revolved loosely around religious beliefs.

Establishing Communication Channels

Finally, our objectives are met with great care and passion. In order to provide the best way to interact and pass on pre-established knowledge, we must respect individual paces.

There should be a very active communication channel, which can be email or on Slack, MS Teams, or Google Classroom, through which everyone can attain advice from faculty or peers. This help should be quick, useful, and productive. The faculty and students must also be free to communicate among themselves according to their respective necessities.

A calendar of events with dates and content for online classes, working groups, and onsite programs (such as workshops and holidays) must be shared beforehand. Students should know what they have signed up for and anticipate the schedule.

Please have a backup plan in place for a platform in case your email provider does not allow mass mailing. In the case of platforms, the administrators must enroll everyone who wants to participate in the course.

Before going online, ensure that there is a reasonable and majority-acceptable Code of Conduct (CoC) established. CoC is of paramount importance and ensures a healthy environment on online platforms, reflected through all communication media. The facilitators and learners must be able to freely converse and share thoughts, but not with the intention of causing any sort of harm or discomfort to others.

CHAPTER 4

Facilitating Learning in a Community Classroom

Time and engagement; that is shared learning experiences, challenges, and success in real-world settings define a community classroom that requires special attention and expertise not commonly experienced in traditional classrooms. To everyone, the classroom is grown as a community with extensive collaboration among schools (stay) and educators (move). This program provided intentionally diversified learning experiences and also opportunities for authentic and real-world problems to be solved critically in interdisciplinary, multidisciplinary, and special education settings. It was structured to apply successful teaching and learning techniques, with careful attention to students' motivation, needs, and values, considering all stakeholders including parents, guardians, and citizens. By engaging teacher candidates in mutually designed, coordinated activities, along with MSU faculty, graduate students, and undergraduate students and community educators/organizations, the learning understanding was enriched.

To successfully demonstrate students' learning in real-world settings, educators must serve not as the imparters of a specific body of knowledge chosen by experts, but as facilitators of individual and group learning in a community, providing different learning experiences, curricula, and learning activities. It is also crucial for teacher candidates to have enough experiences with teaching various ages, school settings, and diversity within communities, to be able to reflect on their progress more effectively in a community classroom. By allowing for a diverse range of learning opportunities from a biomedical research lab at MSU in the school setting, to podcasting and offering individualized tutoring experiences in diverse settings, to seeing the village (community) raising its children, the program prepared teacher candidates to incorporate the impact of a well-rounded education in their teaching and to be lifelong learners.

Encouraging Active Participation

In school gardens, students can help grow fruits, herbs, and vegetables, and occasionally create budgets or give donations to help. The Adaklu school program provides opportunities for children to manage the resources they use, which in this case is environmentally. Many community gardens can trace their lineage back to school programs, and the success of a program can often be traced to an interested adult who sponsors or supervises a maintenance effort. From our experiences, we learned that very small children at the hours activities liked trash collecting the most, and for making gardens, they loved working with soil. In the schools, the garden activities got more challenging along with the grade of the student, as did programs to educate the children, little by little, so that they could easily and naturally follow the rhythm of a natural tree or school forest with familiarity.

School counseling programs may seem too narrow to mention, but they often involve discipline, attendance, curriculum, and parent programs. A "smart education" program to teach communities about climate change is also effective, as is enlisting local-area college and high school students to help create an education program. Many of these activities are focused on getting children to participate in environmental clean-ups, and the education program involves the entire community, not just the students. In each of these interventions, having an adult lead who wants to be involved is key to their success. The adults not only help make the events a reality, but they also actively participate with the children while emphasizing why their behavior is important and good.

Providing Constructive Feedback

Role-playing is one of the regular tactics. When we are able to emerge or submerge in the persona of another, we often realize that, except for when we are working in a truly vile type/role-play of a truly vile situation (like settler colonialist mentalities normalized with a certain swath of our neighbors in the U.S.), normal human being behavior will not include dogging others for reasons that don't objectively exist. Scenarios are custom-designed to help our child/adolescent scholars feel secure as they reflect upon their connectedness in caring and respectful interactions. Another "purple-ass play" is to critically, but responsibly, present a faux ethical dilemma for our mentees to consider and hash out in a relative way. The faux ethical problem will ideally be interesting enough to be worthy of concern and analysis but it must be firmly made-up to limit the possibility of any harm. Our point with this play is always to design a situation that nudges our youthful students and abs-student near-peers to better understand the many ways in which we might exercise judgment and how to tell how to use the judgment I we exercise in their decisions.

I try to build up a read/write relationship with each mentee by teaching them that I'll be happy to read and respond to what they write if they are willing to read and respond as thoughtfully and constructively as they can to what I write (or offer a written question or comment followed by a sincere inquiry: "Why?" "Do you agree?" "Is the same true for (fill in the blank with a related situation)?" and so on). It's an approach that aligns pretty closely with basic rules of the TEC-Variety Model and that has saved me from many headaches, from haircut photos to harassment situations. When we need a route back to respectful and productive exchanges, we use the "no personal data/no faces/no names" rule, knowing that everyone will eventually calm down and that, when we see a violator boldly or subtly breaking the rule, we'll deal with that effectively with our voices, or by role-playing when direct, one-on-one exchanges are better not to force, or reaching out to the offender and common friends via preserved mods or educators.

Fostering Collaboration and Cooperation

During a 1995 workshop of the Mississippi Association of Self-Development of People, presented by Garcia, Jackson, and Pulido, Christine Pulido, an elder in the Hispanic/Latino community in Northern Virginia, talked about the tradition of "mingas." A tradition within Hispanic/Latino culture, the "mingas" is an interdependent process of working for mutual benefit. Traditionally, the minga is called by a member of the community and the community gets together to help this person complete a task. The minga is always associated with joy and celebration. One is essentially thanking the community for having shared in the work and asking that further work be achieved in a similar form. Each future benefactor will in return, at the appropriate opportunity, carry out their work in a similar fashion. Through this sense of community service, a spirit of sharing, cooperation, and the culture of the minga is maintained. This is the attitude we want to instill in our students. It is specifically addressed in our commitment to the "cool down": how we return the classroom to its original state at the end of the week and celebrate our efforts. We often needed to remind and in some cases cajole the students to join in the efforts. By the fourth week, we observed individuals taking responsibility and even team leadership of their groups in volunteering to help others who had not completed the "cool down" task. This process specifically fosters cooperation.

Fostering cooperation: The physical design of the classroom encourages individual and group work. Each table and cabinet stores tools, classroom materials, and individual items that are shared among the group. Each group has elected a tool manager; this student is responsible for keeping the table clean and organized. "Our number one tool is a broom," said an empowered fifth grader. Students are developing a culture of sharing and are beginning to build a cooperative community.

CHAPTER 5

Assessing Learning Outcomes

The survey was repeated each year in May and once again in September 2015, when we conducted a detailed endline survey with the male and female students from the 4th to the 7th standard. Our survey team covered six schools a day, and by the end of the twelve days, we had collected a vast amount of data regarding the learning outcomes, attendance records, and had two meetings with the teachers, guardians, and the students – a brief one before assembly ended and a lengthier one after the children were dismissed for the day. We were gratified to see that 37.7% or 3,557 of the 9,456 students the teachers had identified for our surveys returned after a sixteen-month absence.

In June 2011, a baseline survey was conducted at all twelve schools. It covered both the male and female students from the 4th to the 7th standard, the male and female teachers, the school facilities, attendance records of the students, and the nature of the community involvement with the schools.

Assessing learning outcomes was as essential in the community classroom as it was in the other schools. Tutors recorded learning outcomes in detail and maintained a detailed database of the students' academic progress outcomes of all the subjects at the end of each year. It was these detailed accounts that guided the tutors when holding quarterly meetings with the male and female teachers of the primary and middle schools and at the staff meetings. I also visited the schools regularly and interacted with the teachers and students.

Utilizing Formative Assessments

In May 2017 we came together to write our formative unit assessments for the upcoming year after being inspired by our completion of seventh grade algebraic rigidity. We then gathered in late August of the same year to do the same with our Smarter Balanced Interim assessments. Administrators were also included in the conversation about what each interim assessment was evaluating to better inform the building plan and type of supports the teachers might need. Each assessment was that they accurately reflect unit goals, be complete enough to show a spectrum of learning and disconnects meant to be corrected before the formal examination, and be at a level (measured by the cognitive complexity of the SBAC or Webb's DOK) that would encourage learning without the need for a "one size fits all scaffolding". A bonus that was not discussed directly was that we reduced our grading load too. By using common assessments (effectively creating a common plan across at least two teachers) students are able to learn in several conditions, effectively increasing time learning and lowering teacher workload.

Formative assessments are crucial for individualized instruction, returning to earlier topics as they are touchstones for future concepts, and setting our students up for success. Up until 2016 when some of us joined forces, we looked for and created our own formative assessments because we found common assessments problematic. We began to share the work we were doing, streamline our use of common assessments so they were at their optimal formative state, and write new check-ins together. Coming up with a formative assessment system that worked for all (or at least many) of the teachers our students would see in a given day, a principal, and we teachers was challenging. As a set of teachers, we came up with goals that focused on quality assessments. Searching for and writing our upcoming seventh grade algebraic rigidity unit helped lay the groundwork for future unit plans and the math goals shared across the seventh grade floor.

Promoting Self-Reflection

When students engage in extempore reflection, a minimally-summed affective emotion (what we might call joy) arises, which lasts for a finite length of time, encouraging students to want to engage with the material further and more frequently. This affective response, in effect, acts as a positive feedback loop, enhancing the learning experience being offered. In stark contrast, reflection that is subject to external endorsements (e.g., a peer or instructor requirement) is far less likely to generate this positive feedback loop. If such an endorsement is removed, it exposes the student to undertakings that no longer have any meaning, which, in contrast, ends in a transient period of happiness followed by a renewed sense of frustration, failure, or struggle.

Self-reflection is the primary means for a person to grow and develop both intellectually and emotionally. Moreover, a person who regularly reflects on his or her actions and experiences is generally happier, with enhanced self-esteem. Research has demonstrated that students' levels of happiness invariably rise when they are engaged in a meaningful process of discovery that promotes self-reflection. The ability to engage in this process, of course, is one of life's essential skills, and it is not something that should be taught in isolation or in only one specific version. The community classroom is uniquely poised to offer a variety of opportunities to encourage the emotional and intellectual well-being of lifelong learners. One of the more effective tools we can utilize for our own self-improvement and personal growth is self-reflection.

Evaluating Individual and Group Progress

Though we can offer only an inferred partial quantitative summation of student success for mathematics, science, and high school grades, we can offer an explicitly qualitative summation of student success through our students' exhibitions. Our students' exhibitions are our yardsticks for charting the vital "development of the whole child". Recognizing the withdrawals from program participation of students who are less open to demonstrating their hard work and of those who have had a need to reduce family expenses with tuition to private junior high schools, we can describe how our community classroom system supports the home-school partnership and the three Ps (home-school professional) trajectory throughout the curriculum regardless of beneficial factors that cannot be sustained. In the following three sections, we view stand-alone and interrelated methods for evaluating and reporting the success of all our students' year-long education.

Given this strong emphasis on student inquiry and conversation and the interrelatedness of every one of our units, grading each student three times per year on content mastery of specific subject area standards is unrealistic. Were we to "sanction" and possibly support forwarding students with twos with the same frequency as students with threes in a particular subject, we would routinely need to justify such actions to district and outside groups. Therefore, we rely on our CC community trusting our professional judgment and questioning us when the final grade is not in alignment with the child's abilities as demonstrated by the child's communicative and creative abilities across the curriculum. It is this ongoing communication with parents and students that is essential due to the less regulated, student-centered approach of a community classroom but is missing from a teacher-centric, standard-based approach still very much supported in the traditional setting. Clearly, measuring growth in areas emphasized at CC, but overlooked in traditional schools, is essential. We rely both on student exhibitions and journals to measure these skills. To date, because of the overwhelming parent satisfaction with the program, as indicated through school and district-wide evaluations, our students have maintained during our seven years at CC 100% retention through graduation, the highest language arts MCAS scores on the high-school tenth grade test, and similarly high passing grades in both math and science.

CHAPTER 6

Overcoming Challenges in Community Learning

In this paper, the researcher, a teacher planning to recede from the classroom on family leave, aimed to put together a program where the author forged partnerships between pre-service, future k-6 teachers at a public, predominantly white institution and multicultural community groups in the locale surrounding the campus. Based on findings from data collected via an ongoing self-study and program evaluations, the author aimed to show the power of establishing university and community partnerships to prepare teachers who intend to instruct in diverse settings. Therefore, in this section the author aims to answer the question, how did partnerships help overcome potential roadblocks to community learning?

There were certainly multiple challenges to face when mounting a community classroom program. The intended mission for community-based learning was also somewhat broad – we aimed to construct a program where multicultural issues were explored within diverse community settings, allowing multiple facets of learner diversity to be explored. For example, we hoped to establish partnerships with a Native American community, African American churches, and local, urban Hispanic communities. Through these partnerships, we hoped to gain insight into the specific challenges faced by each culture so that contents might be developed for a class that teachers in each respective group could use back in their schools. Findings would then be compiled and made available to the greater educational research community. Challenges were expected to come at us from every direction!

Managing Conflicts and Disagreements

Group interaction skills include games which promote reinforcing positive interactions among peers, where peers also need to provide positive feedback. To diminish disruptive behavior in the classroom, alternative and incompatible behavior has been demonstrated to be very successful; if the student is bored and disruptive during science or math lesson, he or she is encouraged to participate in some interacting task like reading to a partner. When this competing behavior is initiated and reinforced, disruptive behavior will disappear. Circle time, where each member actively listens and interacts with others through center activities, sharing favorite toys and pictures of interest, participating in rhymes and songs that can, if the content is in agreement with the rules, the behavior is traded for, are initially planned to become the key strategy to manage disruption during transition times. If a class meets at the beginning of the day for circle time, conversely, and all students are taught skills of opinion exchange, circle participants learn communal routine, and transitions become a part of their schedule.

Conflicts in the classroom will happen; we need to make sure they do not escalate to a variety of additional problems. In the classroom, it may begin with the child making fun of or hitting another in the room. If the conflict is not resolved immediately, violent behavior may be reinforced. At the very least, disrupted learning will result, and the student problem behaviors will likely lead to a decrease in student and parental satisfaction with the classroom. In terms of the situation depicted, the teacher is also a victim of the conflict. To directly teach how to solve conflicts, the same sequence that is used to teach desirable substitute behaviors can be used. This sequence includes: (1) promotion of positive consequences contingent on the desirable conflict resolution behavior, (2) errorless learning teaching strategies, (3) planned reinforcement of the taught skills, and (4) generalization from situations similar to those used during training. For all students, with or without disabilities, skills needed to ignore conflicts in school-appropriate manners are also directly taught. This skill is then added to the array of skills needed to foster friendships among students with and without disabilities. Social skills that are specific to conflict resolution can be increased through circle time; the conflict episode is role-played, and experiences can be discussed, with the teacher's full participation.

Addressing Varied Learning Styles

The principles of flexibility, sensing the needs and interests of the class members, camaraderie, collaboration, support for everyone, promoting the sense of academic responsibility and independence in each individual, and integration, must all be taught and lived by the staff with the individuals' individual experiences in mind. The curriculum is broad based with outstanding educational opportunities and appropriate materials designed to support the classroom philosophy. Our mandate, as a specific model in the continuum for the community classroom, must be to integrate the community and the assets it offers, both human and environmental, into the program. Our goal is to provide our society with individuals who have the educational, practical, and social prerequisites needed to allow them to work, contribute, and live in adult life.

In the community classroom, individuals may be working on a variety of subjects and at varying class levels. Our current classroom consists of individuals who are not enrolled in any other classes and who have a variety of educational needs. Thus, individualized programming is necessary. We must also provide many hands-on experiences; emphasize the process rather than the product in learning; and, to be successful, challenge individuals to think, create, express themselves, and work as independently as possible. Investigative and expository learning, through a process of sequential instruction, is imperative in our environment and must be incorporated in every aspect of the program. Learning to learn is of primary importance and is paramount in the quest to take knowledge and make it one's own.

Balancing Individual and Collective Needs

There are many apparent benefits of having wireless, tech-savvy children and young people, but now we are finding that an overuse of new technology is contributing to problems such as the increase in attention deficit disorder and the decline in the quality of physical encounters between people. Additionally, although there are some genuinely great applications which greatly facilitate the acquisition of knowledge, the more widely employed programs are little more than recycled worksheets from the past. Nothing can replace the successful transmission of positive human qualities and values, and that is where digital technology is likely to fall short. When we talk about 'quality education,' it is important to remember that essential human qualities cannot be taught. They must be 'caught,' and in order for that to happen, they must be freely given.

The approach to learning described here is at odds with the individualized approaches to teaching which are more common, such as distance learning. They are not fundamentally incompatible, but they present some real challenges. In the Union City schools, beginning in Grade 8, each student gets a tablet, and among other things, they can access their homework for their various courses online. The school is a wireless hub, and each student is allowed to use their device in most of their classes, most of the time. Teachers can use a number of software programs designed to facilitate online learning, but not all of them were trained to use the programs. We don't have any evidence yet that this new trend increases proficiency in the use of technology tools, and unquestionably, this new capacity is costly.

CHAPTER 7

Expanding the Community Classroom

We have concluded that limited resources in personnel and extended time allowed for course design, life tests, and the enormous amount of paperwork to support this increasingly complex teaching and review process needs to find models that allow us better to leverage our resources. We refused to reduce the detailed Socratic instruction that has simultaneously motivated and pushed the most advanced students, and we have a profound understanding that the traditional accountability models in higher education need changing. We also believe that, as long as we take religious freedom seriously, churches have needs and responsibilities beyond what we are offering to address. We have been led to form a partnership that uses numerous principles and practices that we have come to love. A course must be available to new students, graduates, and social pastors who are not able to attend a full-time college campus, to both bring the model to thousands of the church's most influential future staff and to help nurture ongoing continuing education programs for a denomination whose 18.1% growth last year among adherents makes us one of the highest growing groups in the country. A one-week, one credit-hour intensive format meaning that the teaching at the graduate level and above must be much more focused than total institutional practice, and it forces faculty, peer, and public servants to provide deep and detailed pre-instructional reflection and information support in order to bring to the table more that can be handled through traditional teaching.

It is not enough to be sensitive to community needs; we have to act on that sensitivity. As an institution, Asbury Theological Seminary, under the leadership of doctoral students, has moved forward in a bold new program. The first two courses were organized each year by a senior student who selected two of the most academically influential faculty available to teach 4-week modules. The senior student, as a teaching assistant, subjects himself or herself in the course to the repeated public critiques of research and teaching excellence, and the final promotion or graduation review is fundamentally a public review of the teaching of the senior student, since students from the more recent classes return to review this process. After two such course offerings, these techniques have proven powerful in many dimensions and the interest had grown, but early indications show that the new course failed to have as much of an academic impact on the senior students as the first two, nor the church consisted as much of the senior students as the first two, nor the church and seminary communities as much in the process as well. It appears that interest from outside of the current senior class is larger than we are able to handle.

Engaging External Experts

At the beginning of our international community partnership work, Christina launched a photography exchange in which students in Uptown each contributed four or five photos that symbolized the concepts of home, family, friendship, and community to think deeply into the deeper themes of the Uptown play. Then, these photographs were sent to South Africa, where the students not only closely read them and reflected on the images but also wrote impressionistic responses into letter briefs addressed to the West Side youth. Plot of ten other city educators and a sustainability expert met for the first time. This routine proved a highly productive and instructive way of involving students in an iterative, participatory action research process of future planning in a real park super fund site.

The "Accessing External Expertise" routine in the "Pedagogy of Partnership Teaching Partners' Toolkit" is a great resource for engaging external experts in your class. After first having thoughtful discussions and carefully articulating the kinds of experts that will best serve as learning partners, the class can start reaching out to bring these partners into community dialogues or other activities. Drawing upon this routine, our community classroom set of activities sometimes venture into more traditional engagement with external experts. Here, we share key goals, pertinent routines, successes and challenges with a few different models for working with experts beyond the class community, as well as findings on the impact of working with these adults. In the sections that follow, we begin by considering what new knowledge is introduced to the community classroom with the entrance of an external expert. We also consider what new instructional moves and learning activities were made possible. Finally, we delve into what students thought about the new form of partnership education, how it changed what they could do, and how it potentially transformed their views about expert-adults and how and what expertise can be.

Involving the Wider Community

The Community Classroom encourages the active involvement of adults and children as a matter of course. Educator trainings and parent workshops are regularly held, children and their parents are encouraged to re-craft play and story tools they have invented, be they pregnant or related to parenting. We attempt to steer clear away from established teaching models and offer work means of learning to be as self-sustainable as possible. To reach this goal, The Community Classroom is on the brink of accessibility and representatives, communication and financial structures, whilst the careful foster creation of a network of adults and children that can enhance further cerebral, emotional and attitudinal exchange.

The Community Classroom is looking for ways to provide more children with these opportunities. We want workshops in all parts of the world to result in growing, self-sustainable 'classrooms' of play and learning that will give a continually increasing number of Catholic and non-Catholic children the chance to grow and develop in a loving, educational, stimulating play environment. It is essential to be attentive to cultures and traditions from which stories and play situations originate, as well as to regional needs and requirements with regard to manufacturing resources and knowledge. These needs and requirements often vary widely among the various exchanges of children's play (and the attendants thereof).

Collaborating with Other Community Classrooms

Anyone that has ever participated in or designed a teleconference meeting can likely attest that it is difficult for a worthwhile or in-depth conversation to be had, or for a satisfying conclusion to be reached when time is of the essence. The 30-minute sessions are something I became accustomed to while working in public schools. After 28 minutes or so, it seemed like I could see the kids' energy starting to "fade" and knew that rezoning into another task wouldn't serve any purpose. During the time as a tutor at the McVoy Family Literacy Center, I recall that there were days when I did some teaching, or at least some story selling, about a short break before we kicked into the next subject. The children I worked with would expand their work schedule by an additional 30 minutes because they became personally invested in their work and didn't look at the shorter time as part of the schedule. While they understood that time was nearing.

Acquiring a network of community classrooms is important. You need to have people to learn from and people to teach. It's essential that everyone has the chance to collaborate with as many people from other community classrooms as possible, as learning from multiple other community classrooms can really offer more insight and open their mind to different working environments. When collaborating with other community classrooms, the session would consist of inviting people from other community classrooms to come in and work with us. We might collaborate on a group project or, if I'm near the starting phase of something greater and we were in the middle of this process, I might "tag them" in where we were in the process. For example, I might reach out to a friend that operates a community classroom in Hawaii and ask them to help me figure out the mesh networking of Arduino boards I was working on. In return, I might see what I could "tag in" and help them on. Although our hour is only 30 minutes long, most will stick around for more than just that time and work with us until we are done, usually over dinner. On another occasion, a college classmate of mine who teaches at the University of Minnesota's College of Education met with us weekly for our during dinner.

CHAPTER 8

Empowering Learners in the Community Classroom

We believe, and early findings from matched comparisons of learning outcomes in several content areas and skills appear to confirm, that the Community Classroom Model is highly effective with children with and without disabilities of any age, in as early as 8 weeks. We are showing that we can empower learners through the provision of the High Leverage Practices in Special Education (CEC, 2012) in at least 3 curriculum areas, but likely in all. The model supports all of our key assumptions, outlined in earlier presentations and publications, and yields additional outcomes beyond those identified earlier. Survey data. Our model of a Community Classroom is based upon principles and assumptions derived from working in homes in developing countries, from developmental practice, from focus groups and surveys with stakeholders, and from the researchers' extensive previous work or review of prior findings on inclusion, literacy, and technology. Each of the short-term goals is designed to address an assumption by maximizing the reciprocal benefits for children, families, staff, and preservice teachers in the model of inclusive service delivery. For each element of the program's operation, reaching the definable short-term goal can improve the quality and effectiveness of the program at various stakeholder interfaces both directly and indirectly, by allowing earlier assumptions to be realized more fully. An implementation map, including the hypothesis and the key variables for the data to be gathered, was prepared for each step in a multi-faceted systematic and ongoing review of the progress, which was highlighted by the collection of data on cornerstone behaviors and attitudinal change goals. Data for the review was to be collected in discrete time periods appropriate for the learning history of each group served/affected by the program. Data was to be analyzed to support a program theory that specified the conditions assumed to be necessary and the anticipated impact of each step within a school, e.g., on collaboration, on staff morale, curriculum adaptability.

A model of community classroom teaching and learning was developed at the University of Vermont (UVM). This model was based in part on the lifelong learning strategies that often organize families in crowded, mixed-age, and mixed-ability housing environments in developing and pre-literate cultures. We wanted to better understand just how such interactions work and the impacts on learning, and to adapt these strategies for use in classrooms serving children with or without disabilities of any age. Realizing the potential for the interactions between peers with and without disabilities, the foundation of many inclusive practices, led us to design and test a "Community Classroom" model. We also realized the potential value of such an inclusive model as we faced a shortage of clinical placements and demands for more field experiences for preservice educators, not less. We decided to grow our own teachers, teachers who were more confident yet flexible as they had greater experiences teaching children with various abilities, learning styles, and needs. We also wanted them to see teaming and collaboration by staff as well as between children with and without disabilities in action, to decode their own confusion and to build the courage to ask for help as needed as they developed their teaching skills.

Encouraging Autonomy and Agency

Throughout the last 14 months, we have had the chance to observe the learning process because children's work is visible and tangible. We have observed that children have naturally developed a communal structure where everyone has a task, contributes equally, learns, and teaches. They have decided what to explore and study, what tools to use, methodologies, and what resources they need. It is evident that they have internalized the idea that all learning happens in community and that they are willing to support themselves to grow their learning community.

At our collective, we don't just trust in learning, we trust in teaching. We believe that learning and teaching are a collaborative process, and that many times mentorship and teaching can and need to happen from all the members in the classroom, regardless of age. We trust that children are capable of thinking. We trust that children are capable of questioning, that they are capable of asking innovative questions that might never come across an adult's mind. We trust that if adults put away the idea that they encompass all knowledge of the world and welcome children's perspectives as equal to theirs, more interesting, groundbreaking questions, ideas, thoughts, and answers might surface. We trust that we do not need to know, nor do we have to dominate a canon of knowledge that we force-feed the children. We trust that we need to have the ability to create an environment that motivates children enough to ask these kinds of questions and the ability to recognize them when they appear.

At Camino a Casa, we trust in the learning abilities and instincts of children. We trust that they will act according to their own age and personalities, and that their will and motivation to learn are human rights. We trust that they will become active members in a community of students and will look out for their own and their colleagues' well-being. We trust in an environment that is able to provide children with tools and the setting to achieve this trust.

Promoting Lifelong Learning

Connected learning for adults and for students that is engaged with schools, children and family matters, particularly literacy, science and math, and linked properly to literacy in the schools offers the potential to improve public education and strengthen struggling communities. The model of the Extended Learning Program that provides basic numeracy skills offers a flexible structure rather than a fixed, definite curriculum; is adaptable to changing human and financial resources; and is designed to help people help themselves and strengthen their community. School districts and other entities can choose to follow the model entirely or adopt isolated components. This program may eventually be seen as a way to fill the void of adult learning that caught some people unawares when the manufacturing plants and other businesses that employed them closed down or shifted overseas.

Lifelong learning is a guiding principle for all community schools: schools and extended-day programs, social services and community-based health services, recreation and leisure activities, community activities, and volunteer work. Schools encourage lifelong learning in adults and students through a range of initiatives. Even more important, community schools promote the ideal that families, young people, and other community members should experience learning together and that they should be encouraged to be learners and educators, transmitters and receivers of knowledge, skills, and wisdom. The overall results are greater parent and family involvement in schools, an extended-day program with diverse services and programs for adults and children, teens and elders, and a virtual clearinghouse for community needs, desires, and opportunities that gets to the heart of actions that create vital communities that are linked to schools and to each other.

Recognizing and Celebrating Achievements

Creating a positive classroom culture needs to involve learning and celebrating progress, development, and positive attitudes to dealing with difficulties. It also means recognizing and protecting those who overcome internal difficulties in themselves and in those willing to learn and develop. Children, our pupils, who struggle to come to terms with their fears to approach new experiences should be the focus of our encouragement in public recognition of success. We need to appreciate and fête the fact that achievements result from continuous work, the effort, and the acceptance of the challenges ahead. In our schools, we believe that both students who have developed their potential and students who struggle with fear, anxiety, and trauma learn and achieve in their path of success. We accept that for everyone the reciprocal exchange hides different results and difficulties. Our rule is: "We praise continuous effort over perfect results".

Praising a child who perseveres is key to helping them continue in the learning journey. It's crucial that they feel the reward of conquering a difficult task, facing their fears, and enjoying the fruits of their efforts. Positive reinforcement is beneficial for children, who become more confident and resilient. Celebrating one's achievements is important to promote perseverance, effort, and success. We celebrate the moment and rightfully so. But the momentary success should also be appreciated as a path created by perseverance, continuous effort, and overcoming difficulties. It is important in the first place because there is no learning without persevering and dealing with difficulties. If we cherish in the first place perseverance and effort, we will not fear difficulties and failures, as they will be just steps toward success.